Jobs Then and Now

Sukie Demers

Series Editor • Mark Pearcy

Firefighters stop fires.

They use **tools**.

Then, they used buckets.

Now, they use hoses.

Doctors help sick people.

Doctors use tools.

Then, they used hand tools.

Now, they use computers.

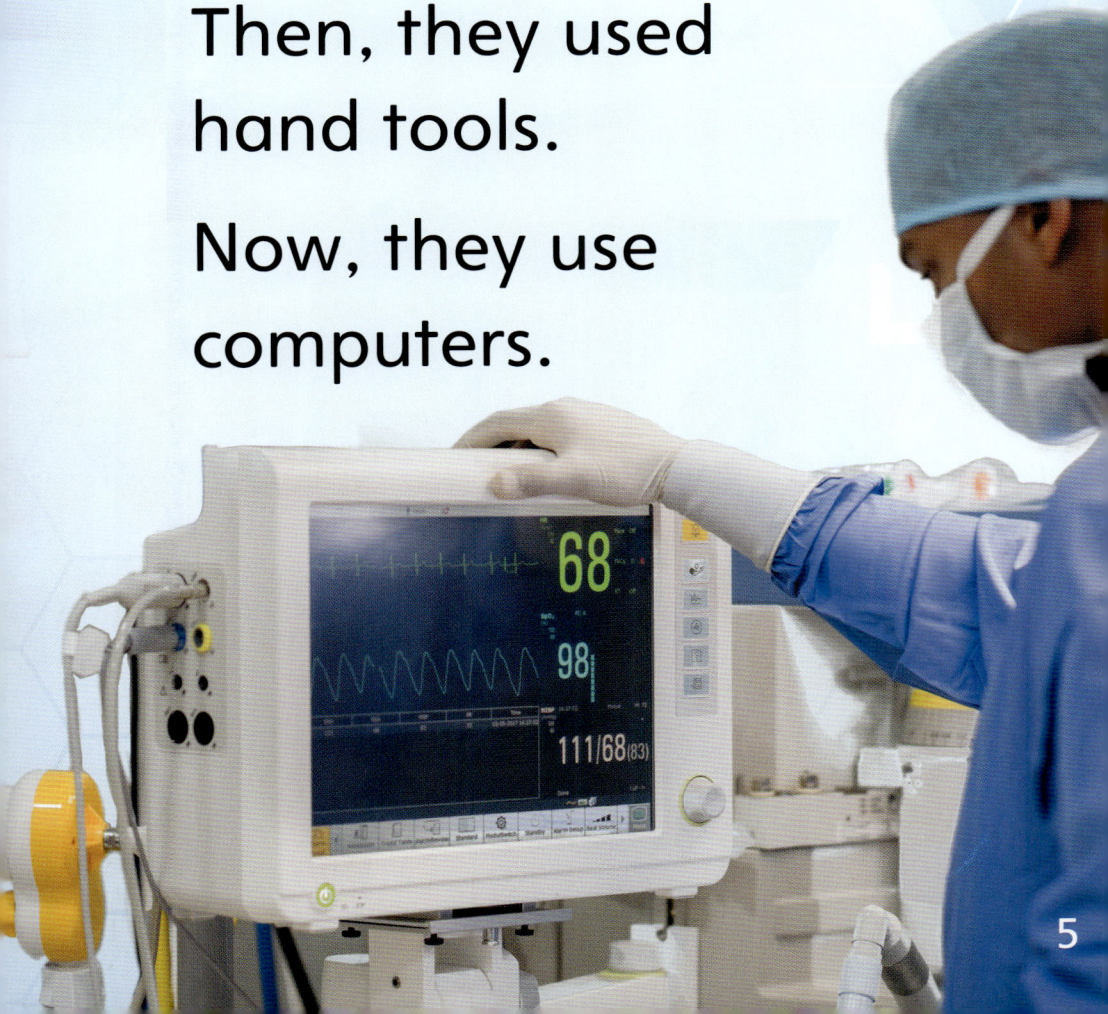

Farmers grow food.

Farmers use tools.

Then, they used animals.

Now, they use tractors.

Teachers help us learn.

Then, they used books.

What do they use now?